THE OFFICIAL RSPCA PET GUIDE

Care for Your
Kitten

CONTENTS

First published in 1986 by
William Collins Sons & Co Ltd, London
New edition published in 1990

Reprinted by HarperCollins*Publishers* 1992, 1994 (twice), 1995, 1996,
1997 (twice), 1998

This is a fully revised and extended edition of *Care for your Kitten*, first
published in 1986 and reprinted in 1988

© Royal Society for the Prevention of Cruelty to Animals 1986, 1990

Text of the 1986 edition by Anna Mews; text revisions and additions for
this edition by Angela Rixon Sayer

Designed and edited by The Templar Company plc
Pippbrook Mill, London Road, Dorking, Surrey RH4 1JE

Front cover photograph: Animal Ark, London
Text photographs: Animal Photography Ltd, Marc Henrie,
Solitaire *(also back cover, bottom)*

Illustrations: Terry Riley/David Lewis Artists and
Fred Anderson/Bernard Thornton Artists

**A catalogue record for this book is available
from the British Library**

ISBN 0 00 412543 6

Printed in Hong Kong by Sing Cheong Printing Co. Ltd.

First things first, animals are fun. Anybody who has ever enjoyed the company of a pet knows well enough just how strong the bond between human and animal can be. Elderly or lonely people often depend on a pet for their only company, and this can be a rewarding relationship for both human and animal. Doctors have proved that animals can be instrumental in the prevention of and recovery from mental or physical disease. Children learn the meaning of loyalty, unselfishness and friendship by growing up with animals.

But the commitment to an animal doesn't begin and end with a visit to the local pet shop. A pet should never be given as a 'surprise' present. The decision to bring a pet into your home should always be discussed and agreed by all the members of your family. Bear in mind that parents are ultimately responsible for the health and well-being of the animal for the whole of its lifetime. If you are not prepared for the inevitable expense, time, patience and occasional frustration involved, then the RSPCA would much rather that you didn't have a pet.

Armed with the facts, aware of the pitfalls but still confident of your ability to give a pet a good home, the next step is to find where you can get an animal from. Seek the advice of a veterinary surgeon or RSPCA Inspector about reputable local breeders or suppliers. Do consider the possibility of offering a home to an animal from an RSPCA establishment. There are no animals more deserving of loving owners.

As for the care of your pet, you should find in this book all you need to know to keep it happy, healthy and rewarding for many years to come. Responsible ownership means happy pets. Enjoy the experience!

Terence C. Bate

Terence Bate BVSc, LLB, MRCVS
Chief Veterinary Officer, RSPCA

Introduction

Kittens are among the most charming of all young animals. Cuddly, playful and enchanting to watch – few people can resist them. However, it's important to remember that kittens need house training, can be very destructive to carpets and furniture, and where there are young children or elderly folk in the family can cause accidents or even get trodden underfoot.

Although a kitten is a very adaptable animal and generally soon makes a good household pet, it does have certain minimum requirements. So before you get a kitten it's worthwhile asking yourself a few basic questions, to make sure it really is the right pet for you.

Kittens are very active, agile and inquisitive.

- Do you have a garden or safe access to the great outdoors?
- Are you at home for at least part of the day, every day?
- Are you willing to put up with the possible damage that claws can do to furnishings?
- Are you willing to bear the cost of vaccinations and possible veterinary attention? The RSPCA strongly recommends that insurance be taken out to cover some of these veterinary costs. (All but those cats kept specifically for breeding should be neutered at about six months of age, and all kittens and young cats should be vaccinated against feline infectious enteritis and feline influenza, which require booster vaccinations throughout their lifetime.)
- Are you willing to pay for boarding your cat when you go on holiday, or have you caring neighbours who would feed and look after it for you? Please remember, however, that on health grounds boarding a kitten is not recommended until the animal is at least six months old.

The answer to all of these questions should be a resounding 'yes'. If you cannot answer 'yes' to them all (and honesty is very important here), please think very carefully before you get a kitten.

Pedigree or mongrel?

Once you are quite sure a kitten is the right pet for you, the next decision to be made is whether to choose a pedigree or mongrel.

For most people, the mongrel or kitten of mixed breeding is the first choice. Generally speaking, these cost little or nothing to buy (many people are only too willing to give a kitten to a good home), but don't forget, of course, that as they grow up they will cost just as much to feed as any pedigree cat. And, naturally, they will need the same amount of love, care and medical attention.

Mongrel kittens are generally hardy, of strong constitution and come in a wide variety of colours and types. The choice is yours.

If you want to know what your animal will look like as it grows up, a pedigree kitten might be the right answer for you. Some breeds have well-known characteristics, like the Siamese with its distinctive voice, or the Longhairs with their dense coats, which require meticulous grooming. Pedigree kittens are, of course, expensive to buy.

However, whether you decide on a pedigree or a mongrel kitten, it's sensible not to take home one which is younger than seven or eight weeks as kittens need to stay with their mother until this time. It's always wise to take a new kitten to your veterinary surgeon for a check-up.

Mongrel

Pedigree: Chinchilla

Which sex to choose?

When deciding which sex to choose, it's worth remembering that male kittens will mature at about the age of six months and from then on, unless castrated, will show a tendency to fight, wander and spray an unattractive scent around the place. Female kittens mature at about the same age, and will then come into season from spring onwards, every two to three months for about eight months of the year. So unless you turn your home into a high-security prison, they will almost certainly become pregnant and produce many litters.

On the whole, therefore, unless you plan to buy a pedigree cat and breed, it's more sensible to have your kitten neutered, whether it's male or female. Neutering is a straightforward operation for your veterinary surgeon to perform. It is not cruel. It is not unfair to the cat. For the vast majority of people who want a kitten primarily as a pet, it is the practical and responsible thing to do (see Neutering, opposite).

It is, of course, simpler and therefore less expensive to neuter a tom than a female. If you do intend to neuter, you'll find that the differences in character between a male and female are minimal after the operation has been carried out. Once neutered, there is often more variety between individual animals than there is between the sexes. Whether you decide on a male or female is a matter of personal choice.

Female kitten

HOW TO TELL A MALE FROM A FEMALE

Sexing a kitten is easier to illustrate than to describe. If you look closely at the illustrations here, you will see that the distance between the anus and the urinary tract opening is very short in a female, and rather longer in a male. Moreover, the opening tends to be slit-shaped in females and rounded in males.

Probably the simplest way to sex a kitten is to lift it on to a table, raise its tail and compare it closely with these two drawings.

Male kitten

Neutering

The RSPCA strongly recommends that any cat which is to be kept as a household pet should be neutered. In the Society's view, it is in the best interests of both cat and owner. The exception, of course is if you have a pedigree kitten which you intend to show and later use for stud purposes.

Some people take the view that it is 'unnatural' to neuter a kitten and believe it will adversely affect its character or its weight. Others feel that it is wrong to deny the animal its basic instincts.

It can be safely said, however, that neutering will not make your kitten overweight when it grows older, unless it is regularly overfed, nor will it have a detrimental effect on its character. As for basic instincts: too frequent matings can result in a tired and overworn female and a tom battle-scarred and sometimes badly wounded from fights over queens.

It's worth remembering that a female will come into season about every two or three weeks for around eight months of the year. As time goes on, it will become increasingly difficult to prevent her from becoming pregnant – and just as difficult to find a first-class home for every kitten.

Many thousands of unwanted cats and kittens are destroyed each year, so it is obviously wiser to spay your female.

Male kittens can be castrated when they are about six months old. This will stop them spraying unpleasant tom cat scent everywhere, wandering off after females and disappearing for days at a time. It will also prevent them from fighting and being afflicted with the attendant injuries – which might well need veterinary attention.

Female kittens can be spayed from about the age of five months onwards. Spaying usually costs more than castrating a male, but it is also a routine operation for your veterinary surgeon to perform and has no harmful effects on the kitten.

Breed varieties

Golden Persian

Blue Point Birman

British Blue

Pedigree cats are usually divided into the following groups: Persian or Longhair, Semi-Longhair, Shorthair, Foreign Short-hair and Oriental.

PERSIAN OR LONGHAIR
Today's long-haired pedigree cats are thought to have originated in Turkey and they were first seen in Europe in the sixteenth century. They were called Angora cats, after the old Turkish city of that name (now called Ankara). Other long-coated cats were brought from Persia and from the descendants of these two types we now have a wide range of **Persian** or Longhair varieties from which to choose. Persian cats have round, broad heads, short, wide noses, large, round eyes, and tiny, tufted ears. Their bodies are chunky and set on thick, short legs with large, round paws. The varieties are named after the coat colour, so Persians may be Black, White, Blue, Chocolate, Lilac, Red or Cream; and also Tabby, Tortoiseshell and a range of bi-colours including Blue and White and Red and White. In addition, varieties have been bred with 'tipped' guard hairs a different colour from the undercoat, giving rise to a range of beautiful effects such as Chinchilla Golden, Shaded Cameo and Black Smoke. Persian cats with 'Siamese' colouring are called **Colourpoints** and are available in the whole spectrum of point colours.

OTHER LONGHAIRS: SEMI-LONGHAIRS
Other long-haired breeds and varieties exist but are less extreme in their features than the Persians, have longer, slightly finer bodies and, often, rather less luxurious fur.

The **Birman** has 'Siamese' colouring, but also has pure white paws and lower legs. The **Ragdoll** also has 'Siamese' patterning and various white markings are called for in show specimens. **Maine Coon** cats came from the United States and are an old breed, long-haired and with a very wide range of permitted colours and patterns. The **Turkish Angora** is also found in a large range of colours, while the

Turkish Van, often called the swimming cat, is white with patches of auburn or cream on the face and tail.

Balinese cats are long-coated versions of Siamese, and should have the same characteristics, while the **Somali** is a long-coated variety of the well-known Abyssinian cat.

SHORTHAIRS

The **British Shorthair** is similar in bodily conformation to the Persian, but it has a very short, dense coat. The colour range is very similar to that of the Persian, with the addition of a range of beautiful spotted varieties.

The **Exotic Shorthair** is a short-coated version of the Persian and is, in fact, bred from Persian and British Shorthair parentage in a large range of colour varieties.

The interesting tailless **Manx** cat, which originated in the Isle of Man is a short-haired variety found in a wide range of colours. (There is also a long-haired variety of Manx which is called the **Cymric**.)

The **Scottish Fold** is similar to the British Shorthair in size, shape and colour, but is distinguished by its forward-folded ears, which give it the appearance of wearing a bonnet.

Although long-haired cats need regular grooming, kittens like this Black Persian can prove irresistible.

The attractive markings of a
Silver Tabby

FOREIGN SHORTHAIRS

This group covers a wide variety of quite different breeds,
though they all tend to be slim and lithe, with longer faces
than the British Shorthairs, and with large ears and long,
fine tails.

The **Abyssinian** has a uniquely ticked coat and is
thought to resemble the cats of Ancient Egypt. The **Rus-
sian Blue** is a beautiful slate grey in colour, with a short,
dense coat, upright ears and green eyes, while another
breed of the same coat colour, the **Korat**, has a different
coat texture, and a heart–shaped face.

Burmese cats come in a whole range of coat colours and
are renowned for their very short, glossy coats. The eye
colour in Burmese should be yellow or gold. **Burmilla**
cats, bred from Burmese and Chinchilla Persians, have
beautifully tipped coats which seem to sparkle, while the
Bombay, bred from Burmese and Shorthaired Black,
looks like patent leather.

Rex cats are curly-coated. There are two main breeds,
named after the English counties in which they were first
discovered. The Cornish Rex, very long, lithe and Oriental

Chocolate Oriental Spotted Tabby

in appearance, usually sports a luxuriantly curled coat, while the Devon Rex has a different body structure, and a soft, wavy coat.

ORIENTALS

The term 'Oriental' in cats covers the **Siamese** and those short-coated varieties derived from Siamese. All these cats should be slim and lithe, with wedge-shaped heads, large pointed ears, long, slim legs and long, pointed tails.

They are intelligent, inquisitive animals. Siamese have their coat colour restricted to the 'points': the face, or mask, the ears, legs and paws, and the tail. All Siamese have blue eyes. The original Royal Cats of Siam were pale fawn with very dark brown/black points, and were called Sealpoint. There are now many colour varieties, some of which occurred naturally, and some produced by selective breeding. Siamese-derived Orientals have lost the gene which restricts the colour to the points, and along with that gene, the one responsible for the blue eye colour. Orientals are found in the same colour range as the Siamese, but generally have brilliant green eyes. The **Oriental** or **Foreign White**, however, is pure white and has deep blue eyes.

Sealpoint Siamese kittens

Biology

Eyes   All kittens are born with their eyes closed – their eyes begin to open when they are from 5 to 10 days old, depending on the breed. To begin with, all kittens have blue eyes; their adult eye colour will not start to emerge until around 12 weeks. Cats have a wide variety of eye colour, ranging through orange, copper, yellow, hazel, green and blue (as in some white cats and in Siamese). A kitten does not see as well as an adult cat until it's around 3 months old, but from then on vision becomes perhaps the most important of the cat's senses.

Teeth   Kittens are born with 'baby' teeth. These start to be shed around the age of 12 weeks, and their full set of 30 teeth have generally grown in by about 7 months. By this age the kitten will have become a young cat and will have a set of 12 incisors, 4 canines, 10 premolars and 4 molars. A cat's teeth should be checked regularly for build-up of tartar and, if this has developed, the cat should be taken to the veterinary surgeon for them to be scaled.

Full set of teeth

Whiskers   Kittens are generally born with a full set of whiskers. They usually have about a dozen whiskers on each upper lip plus a few on each cheek, as well as tufts over the eyes and bristles on the chin. Whiskers grow from hair follicles which are well supplied with nerve-endings so they are very sensitive to touch. Because the extent of a cat's whiskers, from one tip to the other, is the same as the maximum width of its body, they probably provide the means whereby a kitten or cat can judge the width of an opening.

Tail   The tail has many uses. It acts as a balancing mechanism when the kitten is climbing and jumping; provides warmth when it's sleeping; and, very importantly, it is a signalling device. The tail upright and waving cheerfully is often the way a kitten will greet its owner. But the tail fluffed out and twice its normal size is a means of indicating both alarm and warning. When a small kitten's tail becomes giant-sized in the presence of a strange dog, the dog should probably watch out.

Claws   A kitten's claws are a crucial part of its defence system. They are also a weapon of attack and an important aid to climbing. Made of keratin, the horny protein that forms the outer layer of the epidermis, the claws are part of the skin, not the skeleton. A kitten's claws should not usually need to be trimmed – normal healthy usage will keep them the proper length. Only the front paws have a dew claw.

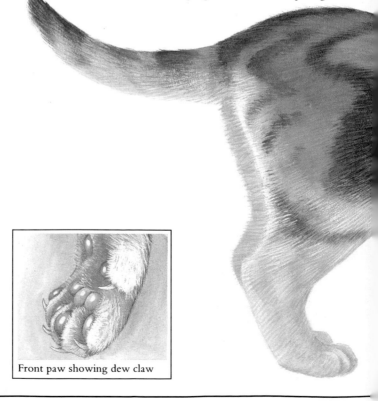

Front paw showing dew claw

Tongue The tongue is an essential aid to effective grooming. A kitten's tongue is long, muscular and very mobile, and the middle of it is covered with small projections, or papillae, which give it the characteristic 'emery board' feel. The tongue is also vital for lapping milk or water, which the kitten should be able to do from about 4 weeks of age. When lapping, the tongue becomes spoon-shaped, and the kitten swallows after about every four or five laps.

Spoon-shaped tongue

Expressing alarm

Ears A kitten has super-sensitive hearing, although white kittens (especially those with blue eyes) do have a tendency towards congenital deafness. Most of the kitten's ear is hidden within the skull bones. The pinna, or ear flap, simply funnels sound waves down to the ear drum, which passes them to the inner ear. A kitten's ears are also a valuable means of expressing anger, fear and pleasure. For instance, the ears of an angry kitten are usually upright and furled back, but a happy and interested kitten has pricked up, perky ears. Later on, the ears play an important part in the animal's social life, especially when courting.

Movement A kitten's skeleton is specially developed to provide extraordinary flexibility. This is achieved by means of an ultra-mobile backbone which enables the kitten to enter all kinds of postures. For example, a kitten can arch its back into an upside-down U; bend itself in half; sleep in a circle; and rotate the front half of its spine while the back half remains stable. By the time a kitten reaches physical maturity, at around 7 or 8 months, it is generally able to jump up to five times its own height.

Kittens are very flexible

Picking out a healthy kitten

Whether you choose a pedigree or mongrel, male or female, you will still want a strong, healthy kitten. If you follow these simple guidelines you should be able to pick out a healthy youngster. So, look for:

1 A nicely rounded animal   Kittens should feel plump and *must be at least seven or eight weeks old* before they leave their mother. Avoid skinny kittens or those with distended tummies. Such kittens are likely to be infested with intestinal worms.

2 Bright, clear eyes   Do not be tempted to take kittens with runny eyes or sneezing noses, or which have a noticeable 'third eyelid' (see p.32).

3 Dry, clean tail   Reject any kitten with a sore anus, wet tail, or diarrhoea, indicated by yellow stains on the fur.

4 A healthy coat   Do a quick check for fleas – many kittens have them and their presence is indicated by small black grits in the fur at the base of the ears, and on the spine towards the tail, as well as on the tummy. These can be dealt with quite easily, (see p.40).

A further word on coats. Remember that a fluffy kitten will almost certainly grow up to be a long-haired cat, and long-haired cats, make no mistake, need a regular daily brush and comb if they are not to suffer from matted coats and dangerous hair balls (see page 24). If you haven't got time to spend grooming a long-haired cat, for goodness sake don't get a fluffy kitten, no matter how appealing it may be. It's much better to go for short-haired varieties, as their coats are a great deal easier to look after. Some short-haired kittens do have a slightly fluffy appearance to begin with, by the way, which can be a little misleading. However, if the mother is short-haired and the father is thought to be, you can be fairly certain your kitten will grow up to be a short-haired cat.

5 Clean ears If a kitten has signs of dry, dark grey deposits in its ears, it's probably affected by ear mites. Your veterinary surgeon can easily deal with this problem, but you ought to be aware of their existence.

The best place to obtain a pet kitten is from friends, or by answering advertisements in the local paper. It is a good idea to see the litter with the mother cat when you make your choice, so you can ascertain that the complete family is healthy and well-cared for. Kittens are often available in pet shops, but those for sale may have come from more than one source and they could have an infection. Such kittens might also have been taken away from their mother before having been completely weaned, which causes digestive problems.

Pewter, Smoke and Shaded Silver Persian kittens: the choice can be bewildering if you decide upon a particular breed. Books, local clubs and breed societies will all offer advice.

Housing

COMFORTABLE SLEEPING QUARTERS

Kittens spend a great deal of time asleep and do need plenty of rest, so a warm, dry, comfortable bed is essential. Cardboard boxes, especially deep-sided ones (to keep out draughts), make useful beds. They can be lined with newspaper, which is warm, inexpensive and easily changed. It is also possible to buy wicker cat beds, or ones made from durable plastic which are easily cleaned.

That said, it's more than likely your kitten will choose some other place for its afternoon nap, and give no more than a passing sniff to the bed you've prepared. Don't worry – this is just an example of a kitten's independent nature. However, if there is a place where you really don't want your kitten to sleep (on your bed, or on a baby's, for example), then you must firmly shut the door and make that room inaccessible.

Cardboard box bed

LITTER TRAYS

House training is the first lesson every kitten needs to learn. Fortunately, most of them are instinctively clean.

You will need to provide your kitten with a leak-proof tray or box (plastic or enamel is best), which should be about 40 × 25cm/16 × 10in, and put it in some convenient corner. The tray can be filled with sand, peat, dry earth or the sort of cat litter you can buy from any pet shop or most large supermarkets. The sides of the tray need to be high enough to stop litter being scattered about by over-zealous kittens. In fact, some people find a large washing-up bowl makes a good litter tray, as it has deep sides and can be easily scrubbed out. Hooded litter trays are available, and these provide ideal facilities for kittens which like their toilet arrangements to be private.

Hot water and soap are all you need. Bleach can be used from time to time, provided it is thoroughly rinsed away, but avoid household detergents, many of which contain coal tar and carbolic derivatives which can be dangerous to kittens and cats.

Litter tray

A cat flap provides a kitten with freedom and independence.

It's a good idea not to empty the tray completely each time but to add a little of the old litter to the fresh, at least until the kitten is completely house trained. A litter tray must be kept clean and must be emptied regularly, otherwise the fastidious kitten will simply refuse to use it.

If you should be unlucky enough to find a few accidents on your carpet, a spray of plain soda water can help to remove the smell, and there are several effective proprietary brands of stain remover available.

If you have a garden to which your kitten has access, you will probably find that in time the kitten will tend to go outside, in preference to the litter tray (in warm weather, at least). If there are areas in the garden that are forbidden to the kitten – new seed beds, for instance – these are best made inaccessible by the use of chicken wire or some form of netting.

A CAT FLAP GIVES INDEPENDENCE

Until your kitten has reached the stage where it really knows its way around the house and the garden, it is best not to let it out without some kind of supervision.

Once a kitten is confident of its home and surroundings, and has been fully immunized, a cat flap fitted to an outside door will provide the freedom and independence cats enjoy. It is important to fit the cat flap correctly and at the right height, and to teach your kitten to use it correctly. The spring should be strong enough to close the flap, but not so strong as to trap the young cat's head or tail as it passes through. There are several types available which can be bolted or set to open in only one direction.

If necessary, older cats may wear a radio-controlled device on a collar which opens a specifically designed cat flap, and prevents entry by stray cats.

The majority of cat injuries occur at night, so although your kitten is probably liveliest at night and might want to stay out, it's wiser and safer to make sure it's inside. Town cats or kittens, especially, should be kept indoors after dark and given a litter tray.

It is possible to keep a kitten or cat without allowing it to go outside, but a number of difficulties can arise and, unless there are exceptional circumstances, the RSPCA does not recommend keeping a kitten or cat in this way. Restricted living conditions often lead to boredom, which in turn encourages destructive habits like carpet-ripping and furniture-scratching.

Introducing the new kitten

TRAVELLING COMFORTABLY

Before you bring home a new kitten, it's sensible to carry out some advance preparations which will make life more comfortable both for the kitten and the family.

First of all, you'll need some kind of travelling basket in which to transport the kitten. These range in quality from the cheapest cardboard carrier to the more expensive wicker or wire variety. Whichever you choose, it should measure at least 50 × 28 × 28cm/20 × 11 × 11in. A travelling basket is a good investment for every cat owner, since it will be essential for taking your kitten to the veterinary surgery (for vital vaccinations) as well as all the other occasions when you may need to transport it. Many cats are upset by the confinement and the noise and smell of a car or bus. Accustom your kitten to associating its travelling basket with treats to lessen the ordeal (p.29).

SETTLING IN SAFELY

Once your kitten is safely home, it's best to confine it, for the first few days, to just one room in the house. The room chosen should be free from hazards, such as open chimneys and trailing electrical cables (see pp.36-7). Kittens can and do find their way into the tiniest of spaces and can be very difficult to extricate. There should be no open windows or doors when the kitten first arrives, for even the most placid of kittens may be upset by its first journey into strange surroundings. Make sure that the kitten knows where its litter tray is, and put its bed in a warm, draught-free place.

You could pop a small alarm clock with a loud tick into its bedding. The rhythm of the ticking will remind the kitten of its mother's heart-beat, and may help it to settle down more quickly.

Remember that kittens need lots of rest and sleep; if there are small children in the family be sure to explain this to them. A young kitten, just removed from its mother and brothers and sisters, will not unnaturally be a little home-sick at first, so plenty of care, affection and understanding is

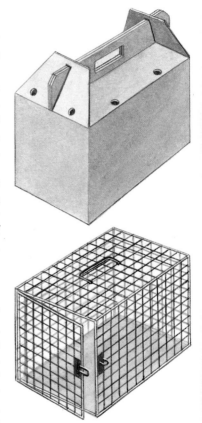

A cardboard pet carrier (top) and a longer lasting basket in plastic-coated wire mesh – light, easy to clean and affording a cat a good view of its surroundings, something many appreciate.

called for. Some kittens, too, are more timid than others, and will need longer to adjust to their new surroundings. If this appears to be the case, don't rush your kitten, but allow it to 'hide away' if it feels like it. It will emerge as soon as it feels more confident.

During the first few days don't allow the kitten to be overhandled by strangers or squeezed too affectionately by youngsters.

FIRST MEETING WITH OTHER PETS

If you already have a dog or another cat in the household, it's important that the first meeting between the newcomer and the resident pet is under strict supervision. It's often sensible to keep the older pet shut up for a while, to allow the newcomer to get used to its scent. Cats and kittens being introduced to one another react primarily to scent, and it is sometimes helpful to rub a little talcum powder into the coats of each animal, under the chin and around the base of the tail.

Most mature animals are tolerant of young ones but occasionally jealousy can turn to aggression. For this reason make sure that introductions take place slowly, with 'retreating' space available for all concerned. Or obtain a mesh play pen to protect the kitten while the established pet learns to accept its presence. Do not let resident pets feel neglected – this may worsen natural jealousy and lead to behavioural reactions such as aggression and persistent attention-seeking.

Dogs and young kittens frequently become great friends, provided first introductions are tactfully made.

Feeding

A sensible feeding programme – which means the right food in the right proportions – is essential to a kitten's healthy growth and well-being. If you are buying a pedigree kitten, the breeder will probably supply you with a specific diet sheet for you to follow.

Feeding regimes vary, but basically you can use prepared tinned food only or a mixture of fresh and prepared food.

Meat meals should always be fed fresh and never allowed to go stale.

USING PREPARED FOOD
Most prepared foods contain all the necessary vitamins and minerals to provide a balanced diet for your kitten. Some contain more moisture than others, and some have a greater concentration of meat. If you use these foods, it is extremely important to *read and follow* the manufacturer's instructions, and feed accordingly.

USING A MIXTURE OF FOODS
You may prefer (and so may your kitten) to use a mixture of foods, giving fresh fish, rabbit or heart several times a week and supplementing this with tinned food or the crunchy, dried kind of cat food, which is very good for the teeth (but do make sure your kitten always has access to plenty of fresh water). Fish and chicken must both be fed properly cooked, and all the bones must be carefully removed. Remember to chop or mince the meat, chicken or fish very finely, as kittens only have 'baby' teeth until they get their adult set at around the age of seven months. Raw meats like heart or rabbit should be cut into thin strips and must be fed absolutely fresh as they can otherwise carry harmful bacterial infections. Do not feed liver, cooked or raw, to your kitten more than once every couple of weeks as too much liver can cause *hypervitaminosis* (a dangerous surplus of vitamin A). Also be cautious about feeding too much lean meat to young kittens, as it can cause a calcium imbalance.

VITAMIN AND MINERAL SUPPLEMENTS
Prepared cat foods already contain a balanced supply of vitamins and minerals, but if you are principally or exclusively using fresh foods, it would be wise to give your kitten a daily yeast tablet, as well as a balanced vitamin and mineral supplement. Your veterinary surgeon can supply these.

FEEDING SUGGESTIONS
At the age of eight weeks a kitten should be independent, and totally weaned from its mother. It must receive small meals at frequent intervals to allow its digestive processes to develop properly. At this age the kitten's stomach is only the size of a walnut.

With a young kitten, under twelve weeks, it's advisable to give five meals a day, each meal consisting of about one tablespoonful of food. Remember that with fresh foods

Feeding chart for kittens from 8–24 weeks

Age (weeks)	Number of 'milk' feeds	Number of 'meat' feeds	Size of each feed (teaspoons)
8–12	2–3	2	3–4
12–16	2	2	6–8
16–24	1	2	9–12
25 +	0	2	12

Grass is essential

Don't forget that all kittens and cats need to be able to obtain a little grass, which they eat to maintain their natural digestive balance. If your kitten is to be denied access to the outdoors for any length of time (say, more than a week or two), it is advisable to put some grass in a pot and keep it inside, by the water bowl.

you must include some cereal in your kitten's diet, so make sure one of the meals has some finely ground breakfast cereal or a spoonful of soaked, brown breadcrumbs in it.

From the age of about twelve weeks, your kitten can go down to four meals a day, and by the age of six or seven months, two meals are quite sufficient. Naturally, as you decrease the number of meals, you must increase the quantity of food in each.

In the chart we recommend 'milk' feeds and 'meat' feeds.

'Milk' feeds consist of any proprietary kitten milk or evaporated milk made up at twice the concentration advised for human babies. If the kitten is intolerant of all forms of milk, try substituting plain yogurt, plain *fromage frais* or cottage cheese. Any acceptable cooked cereal may be added; cats cannot digest uncooked cereals.

'Meat' feeds consist of any good quality cooked and minced or finely chopped meat or fish, raw, scraped meat, or high protein canned meat.

Whatever food is chosen, do ensure that the diet is as varied as possible, and never stick to just one brand of canned food or your kitten may refuse to eat anything else as an adult cat.

NEVER feed your kitten meals straight from the refrigerator; its food should always be at room temperature.
NEVER leave food down. If a meal is not cleared in twenty minutes or so, remove it. Feed less next time.
NEVER feed your kitten on soiled plates. Always wash its dishes in hot water with detergent, rinse well and allow to drain dry. Have a set of dishes just for your kitten's use.
NEVER feed your kitten with fish or poultry bones or skin.

Most kittens enjoy milk, but it should be remembered that this is a food and not a drink to them. Never give milk straight from the refrigerator to a kitten.

NEVER give your kitten squares of meat which may stick across the palate and cause it to panic. Cut raw meat into long, thin, string-like strips.

NEVER try to wean your kitten off meat, even if you are a vegetarian yourself. Cats cannot get all the protein they need from non-meat sources.

Some kittens are much greedier than others and some grow more quickly, so there are many variations in feeding programmes. However, the basic ground rule is 'feed to appetite'. If your kitten is constantly leaving its food, you are possibly giving it too much; if, on the other hand, it is always shouting for more to eat, consider whether or not you should increase its intake (but first look carefully at its condition and do not be taken in by mere greed).

MILK AND WATER

All kittens need constant access to a fresh supply of drinking water. If a kitten does not appear to be drinking enough, it may be because it doesn't like the water (nowadays some of the chemicals in tap water are most unpalatable to cats). If this appears to be the case, try offering clean rainwater, or bottled water.

Milk is not essential for kittens, and indeed some do not like it one bit. It can often cause diarrhoea, so feed it sparingly, if at all. Remember, milk is strictly speaking a food, not a drink.

Fresh water should be available at all times.

Grooming

KEEPING YOUR KITTEN IN GOOD CONDITION

If you were simply unable to resist getting a fluffy-coated kitten, then you must be prepared for regular daily grooming sessions. The sooner these start the better, as kittens are much more amenable to brushing and combing when grooming starts at an early age.

However, all kittens and cats benefit from grooming at certain periods in the year, when their coats begin to moult. This is usually in the spring and, to a lesser extent, in the autumn. It's very important that they should not swallow too many loose hairs when they groom themselves as these matt up in the stomach and form hair balls, which can cause serious illnesses.

Grooming also keeps dandruff to a minimum and, of course, gives you a chance to check your kitten's skin condition carefully, thereby ensuring that any lumps or bumps are discovered and attended to.

BASIC EQUIPMENT

The equipment required for grooming your kitten is very simple. You'll need a soft brush, a wide-toothed comb, a fine-toothed flea comb, and a damp chamois or wash leather.

LONG-HAIRED KITTENS

As already mentioned, long-haired kittens need combing daily, otherwise their fur gets into a nasty matted mess, which is not only unsightly but also uncomfortable and potentially a hazard to health. The fur should be combed through thoroughly, but gently, starting at the head and gradually working back towards the base of the tail, using a wide-toothed comb and combing against the lie of the coat to separate each hair. It is important to groom under the body and around the base of the tail where the hair is extra fine. If grooming is neglected, dense tangles will have to be cut out and very bad cases may need veterinary attention.

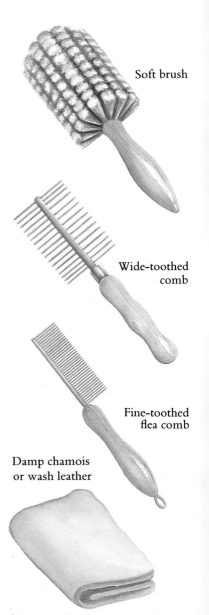

Soft brush

Wide-toothed comb

Fine-toothed flea comb

Damp chamois or wash leather

SHORT-HAIRED KITTENS

Short-haired kittens will certainly need less attention paid to their coat as they can effectively groom themselves, but keep a close eye on them at moulting time. Brushing with soft brush will pay dividends, or you can run a damp chamois leather over the coat to pick up any loose hairs quickly. Just hold the leather in both hands and draw it over the kitten from head to tail. Hand grooming is beneficial to both kitten and owner and helps bonding between the two. Stroke the kitten fairly firmly from head to tail with clean, dry hands.

A kitten with a dull coat or one which moults excessively may not be in the best of health, perhaps due to a poor diet (p.21).

Remember to comb your long-haired kitten carefully each day. Brushing is the final stage in grooming.

Abyssinian

Somali

Chocolate Longhair

Long-haired Brown Tabby

Cream Cornish Rex

Colourpoints

Handling and training

HANDLING A KITTEN OR YOUNG CAT

It's always preferable to pick up a kitten or young cat by putting one hand underneath its chest and the other around its hind legs, so that the animal's entire weight is supported. If the kitten is then turned towards the handler, it can cling to clothing for extra security.

It is never a good idea to pick up a kitten by the scruff of the neck as this puts too much strain on its body and internal organs. (Only mother cats should pick up kittens by the scruff of the neck, and even they only do this when the kitten is very tiny.)

Children will often play with a kitten by picking it up just by its forelegs or even by its tail. Although many cats will put up with much more than ought to be expected, all members of the family should be taught to treat a kitten very gently.

You should accustom your kitten to being handled all over its head and body, particularly if it is long-coated and must be groomed daily. Make handling a pleasure for your kitten by being gentle. Soon the kitten should allow you to look inside its ears and mouth without flinching or trying to bite you. You must exercise patience and combine the serious examination with stroking or scratching the top of its head, areas which are sensitive to touch and will give a pleasurable sensation to the kitten.

Always support the kitten's full weight.

TRAINING

Kittens learn quickly and if you want to train your kitten you will need to start early. You will also need lots of patience! Make sure that training sessions are fun for all concerned. Short and frequent periods of training are better than long ones now and again.

Kittens can be trained to come to call. Put your kitten across the room from where you are and call its name, using a fairly high, clear voice, followed by the command 'come'. When it obeys, make a big fuss of it and offer a small titbit as a reward.

How *not* to carry a cat or kitten!

Perhaps the most important aspect of training is to teach your kitten to go willingly into its carrying box or basket. You should make this a special event by putting a favourite plaything or titbit into the carrier, shut the kitten in for a short while, then open the lid and make a great fuss of it. Turning the carrier into part of a game will pay dividends when you need to take your kitten to the surgery or on a journey.

Some kittens respond to training as 'retrievers' and, with very little encouragement, will chase after and return to you such things as catnip mice, paper balls, and spidery toys made from twisted pipe-cleaners.

As the kitten gets older, you will find that a sharp clap of the hands accompanying the 'no', when it misbehaves, proves a kind, effective method of training.

It's natural for kittens to jump up on high places, scratch furniture and chase birds. If you don't want your kitten to do certain things, you must make that clear from the beginning with a firm 'no'. Remember, however, that although you can train cats not to claw chairs or jump on to the china cabinet, you will not train them to ignore their predatory instincts. Kittens are very sensitive to criticism, so don't be too harsh. Correction should be firm but gentle. Scolding a kitten for any misdemeanour after the event is meaningless – it will simply not understand why you are cross.

A well-cared for kitten should grow into a happy, healthy cat with which you can share years of good companionship.

Exercise

Although kittens have a great deal of energy (like most youngsters), they also need plenty of rest. Your kitten is likely to play furiously for ten minutes or so, and then be more than ready to sleep for several hours. It's very important, therefore, that young children should not try to wake the kitten while it's sleeping.

OUTDOOR EXERCISE

Once you are quite sure your kitten really knows its way around the house, it can be safely let outside to play, provided it can always get back quickly to the security of its home and bed. If you have a fitted cat flap, this will mean that your kitten can always beat a safe retreat if the outside world suddenly looks too alarming.

An opportunity for outdoor exercise is important for kittens.

THE PROS AND CONS OF COLLARS

You might be considering that a collar would be advisable for your kitten, with a tag showing your name and address. A collar is acceptable provided: a) the kitten has no overwhelming objection to it; and b) it is not more than about 1 cm (½ in) wide and is made wholly or partly of elastic.

A collar does, of course, provide a useful means of identification, but it also carries an element of risk as it could get caught on a branch, for example, and the kitten might be unable to escape. While a collar is especially useful after moving house, for instance, it might be wisest to remove it when you feel any danger of your kitten straying is over.

INDOOR EXERCISE

It's a good plan to encourage your kitten to play in the house as well as outside. Provide a selection of suitable toys for it to play with: old cardboard boxes to hide in, cotton reels to chase, and pieces of string to pounce on are all much appreciated, as are newspapers and large paper bags which rustle. Some kittens are particularly keen on toy mice stuffed with catnip. However, be wary of toys made of plastic, as they can be harmful if they are chewed.

Kittens are very fond of playing with feathers. A stiff feather about 12 cm/5 in long will provide hours of fun as the kitten bats it around from paw to paw, tosses it in the air and carries it around, growling. A long feather, such as the tail feather from a peacock makes an excellent decoy, and you can exercise you kitten by getting it to chase the feather tip, moved tantalizingly to and fro across the floor. Do not encourage your kitten to play with man-made yarn which causes intestinal problems if swallowed.

If your kitten is not going to spend a lot of time outdoors, or your garden is short of trees, it might be wise to provide a scratching post – all kittens' claws need sharpening from time to time and this is best *not* done on your furniture and curtains. A simple log kept in a convenient place, or a small post covered with a piece of cloth (some kittens prefer this), will usually be quite sufficient. If despite this, your kitten does show a tendency to head for the furniture, discourage it gently but firmly, and point it towards the scratching post. If you want your kitten to use a scratching post, it's best to encourage it to do so from an early age. Good habits are more easily formed when an animal is young and easily trained.

Scratching post

The healthy kitten

If you do not have a certificate to show that your new kitten has been fully vaccinated, you should make an appointment with your veterinary surgeon, and take your pet along, packed safely in its carrier, at the appointed time. Before administering the vaccine, the veterinary surgeon will thoroughly check the health of your kitten and, depending on the make and type of vaccine used, either one dose, or two doses with a 14-day interval between, may be given. Your kitten should not be allowed to come into contact with other cats which may not be vaccinated until its immunity is complete.

A kitten's health is reflected in its coat, eyes and general demeanour.

The veterinary surgeon will tell you whether or not a course of worming medicine for your kitten is advisable, and may also discuss a suitable date for neutering. He or she will check the teeth, to see that they are all coming through properly and that there is no sign of gum disorder. If you ask, you will be shown how to examine and clean the ears, and how to extend and clip back the kitten's claws.

It is important to establish a happy relationship with your veterinary surgeon while your kitten is in good health. You may need him some day in an emergency situation.

If the kitten is eating normally, and its faeces and urine are passed regularly and are inoffensive, if its eyes are bright, its coat glossy and it is playful and active, then there is likely to be little wrong with its general health.

Signs of illness include loss of appetite, listlessness and an 'open' appearance of the coat, due to the hairs being held semi-erect in an attempt to reduce a raised body temperature.

Cats have three eyelids, the upper lid, the lower lid, and the nictitating membrane or 'haw' which passes across the eye from the inner corner. When a kitten has a raised temperature, or is incubating an illness, the 'haw' is often visible as a film-like skin across the inner corner of the eye. Sometimes teething troubles cause the 'haw' to show, and a quick look inside the mouth might confirm this. Kittens' second teeth often erupt before the milk teeth are shed, and

If your kitten deviates from any of the 'signs of health' listed on p.34 do seek veterinary advice at once. So many cat illnesses and ailments can be cured if they are caught in the earliest stages.

Healthy kittens will find endless amusement in the simplest of props, and love holes and tunnels to jump in and out of.

having both sets present makes the mouth crowded and the gums so sore that the kitten may not want to eat. Giving long strips of raw meat might help the kitten to remove the loose milk teeth. Otherwise they may have to be professionally removed.

The most common problem encountered in an otherwise healthy kitten is diarrhoea, and this is almost always caused by incorrect diet. You may be feeding too much food, it may be too rich, too cold, or just indigestible. If your kitten was obtained from a reliable source you should have been given a diet sheet or details of the food on to which the kitten was weaned, and you should try to continue with the

Kittens at play will act out the stalking, pouncing and fighting of their wild relatives.

same feeding régime for some weeks. Some kittens, especially those with Oriental forebears, are unable to digest whole milk and some dairy products, and in any case of diarrhoea, milk and dairy products should be withheld.

Over-zealous use of some cleaning agents on floors, carpets and litter trays can also cause diarrhoea in young kittens so always take great care in using any chemical products, and make sure that the kitten does not pad around on wet floors or on contaminated soil.

In the garden, keep the kitten away from all forms of chemical fertilizer, soil dressings and slug pellets. Take care that it cannot come into contact with any form of paint or wood preservative. Remember that cats are attracted to the anti-freeze substance used in car engines, though this is lethal to them, and make sure your kitten stays out of your garage.

SIGNS OF HEALTH

Abdomen	without wounds, growths and sores; not distended or unduly sensitive.
Anus	clean, with no staining or scouring; motions passed without persistent constipation or diarrhoea.
Appetite	good; weight maintained with steady growth; no persistent vomiting.
Breathing	even, quiet, with no wheezing or coughing.
Claws	no splits, thorns, splinters or damaged pads.
Coat	clean, well-groomed, glossy; free from parasites, their eggs and droppings, loose hairs and scurviness; no baldness or patches.
Deameanour	watchful, even at rest; quickly responsive to sounds; playful, lively and contented.
Ears	pricked to catch sounds; free of discharge; no irritation, scratching or shaking of the head.
Eyes	clear, not bloodshot; third eyelid (thin membrane that sometimes flicks across the eyes during illness) not showing; no discharge or watering.
Faeces	firm, with no persistent constipation or diarrhoea.
Movement	free movement, agile, with no stiffness in joints or gait; weight evenly distributed.
Skin	supple, with no scurf, inflammation, parasites or sores.
Teeth and gums	clean teeth; gums pink, not inflamed or white or yellowish; no bad breath.
Urine	passed effortlessly with no pain.

Vaccinations

There are many diseases to which kittens and cats are prone, but fortunately two of the most serious illnesses, feline infectious enteritis and feline upper respiratory disease (more commonly known as feline influenza or 'cat flu') can be prevented by vaccination. It is strongly recommended that you have your kitten or cat vaccinated against both these potentially fatal diseases.

FELINE INFECTIOUS ENTERITIS
This is the most serious disease. It spreads so quickly through a neighbourhood, leaving so many cats dead, that people often think there has been widespread poisoning. Young cats are particularly vulnerable, and the disease is at its worst in summer.

The symptoms are a sudden rise in temperature and the refusal of food. The cat sits huddled up, often near a water bowl or sink, without taking water. It vomits occasionally, cries faintly when picked up, and passes blood-stained motions. Death can occur within twenty-four hours.

FELINE INFLUENZA
The symptoms of 'cat flu' are running of the eyes and nose, sneezing, and, later, congestion of the lungs. The cat should be kept quiet and warm, and veterinary help should be obtained at once. Cats may die of this disease, so prompt attention and careful nursing are essential.

A blocked nose is another common symptom, along with a loss of appetite because the cat is unable to smell its food or because it has painful ulcers in its mouth.

Once a cat has had cat flu, it will almost certainly carry the virus in the lining of its nose for the rest of its life.

VACCINATIONS ARE VITAL
At around the age of 12 weeks, kittens may be vaccinated against both feline infectious enteritis and 'cat flu'. Booster vaccinations are needed about every 24 months for feline infectious enteritis and about every 12 months for 'cat flu'.

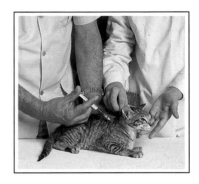

Regular booster vaccinations will give your pet lifelong protection from the major illnesses most likely to threaten it.

Household dangers

Many people keep their kittens confined to the kitchen as this is usually warm and easily cleaned. The kitchen of a normal home is, however, full of potential danger to an inquisitive mischievous little cat.

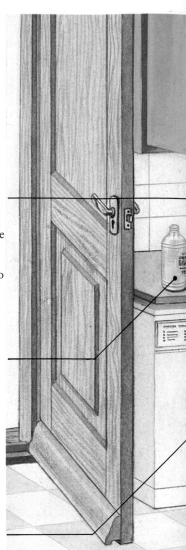

A kitten can become asphyxiated if confined in a room with **inadequate ventilation**, and with a gas or solid fuel boiler burning. Always make sure that your kitten has an adequate source of fresh air if it has to be shut up alone for any length of time.

Most **paints, sprays and solvents** are highly toxic to cats, not only when taken internally, but also if absorbed through the skin or the paw pads. The vapours, being heavier than air, sink to floor level, and so affect pets more than humans, giving rise to a severe toxic reaction.

Kittens find trailing **electrical cables** to be very attractive, pouncing, grasping the flex in all four sets of claws and then biting hard. If live, the wire can give the kitten a fatal shock. Even if switched off and unplugged trailing flex may tempt a kitten to play, and its weight could pull a heavy iron or kettle to fall on to it.

Most household **cleaning products** are toxic to all felines.

A nervous new kitten may crawl into the back opening of the **washing machine, dryer, dishwasher** or **refrigerator**, or may crawl through any hole in the back of a kitchen cupboard and become trapped. Attracted to the warmth, kittens have been recorded as climbing inside washing machines and dryers and curling up to sleep. If unnoticed, the machine could be switched on with fatal results. **Chimneys** are notoriously attractive to kittens.

Hobs and hotplates Kittens have been scalded with liquids from pans and kettles in the best-managed of kitchens. Even when switched off, hotplates can burn delicate paw pads.

A kitten will be fascinated by trailing **sewing thread or wool**. Once it starts to swallow a length of thread it is unable to pull it back out of the throat. It will keep swallowing until the needle is either wedged in the mouth or itself swallowed, when emergency veterinary treatment will be needed.

Kittens are naturally attracted to the dangling leaves of **house plants**. Many species are poisonous, so keep well out of reach.

Ailments

ABSCESSES
With a long-haired kitten, daily combing will quickly show up any abscess, swelling or wound which may be hidden in the long fur, and for which veterinary treatment might be needed. With short-haired kittens, daily observation and handling should reveal any wounds that might need expert handling.

ALLERGIES
Allergies are fairly common in kittens and have a variety of causes. Some kittens are allergic to milk and dairy products (see p. 22) while in others, fish may cause a dry and irritating skin condition along the base of the spine. Parasites such as fleas can initiate a similar irritating eczema, particularly in the warm summer months. Houseplants, household cleaning products, sprays and some man-made fibres may be responsible for making your pet ill. Any persistent diarrhoea, vomiting or discarge of the eyes could point to an allergy, and a complete veterinary check is advisable.

DIGESTIVE COMPLAINTS AND HAIR BALLS
In slight cases of these troubles, the kitten will provide its own remedy by eating grass. It's therefore very important for town kittens or cats to have access to grass, even if it's only in a window box or specially grown in a flowerpot. Occasional constipation can be relieved by a tablespoonful of medicinal paraffin or olive oil (half a tablespoonful for a kitten under six months), which can be repeated twice daily for two days. For any more serious digestive upset, like persistent vomiting, veterinary advice should be sought at once.

EAR PROBLEMS
There are different causes for what is often referred to as 'canker' of the ear, and only your veterinary surgeon can make a diagnosis and give the appropriate treatment. There may be a foreign body (a grass seed, for example) in the ear,

although a common cause of ear trouble is the presence of a mite which lives and breeds in the wax deep down in the ear. If your kitten or cat shakes its head in pain and scratches its ear, seek veterinary help straight away as the ear is extremely delicate.

EYES

If you suspect your kitten might have an eye problem, take it to your veterinary surgeon immediately. The first signs will often be a weeping eye, or one that is swollen or partly closed. Sick kittens will sometimes show the third eyelid, which looks like a film across the eye.

SKIN DISEASES

Most kittens and young cats are healthy and resilient. Keeping them that way can best be achieved by good diet, exercise and careful observation.

If sore or bald patches or pimples appear on the kitten's skin, veterinary help is needed. It is dangerous to apply medication (ointment, for instance) without veterinary advice, since the kitten may well be poisoned by licking it off. Besides, there are many different causes of similar-looking conditions. There may be mange or ringworm, which are serious if neglected but easily cured by the right treatment.

Skin problems can also be caused by fleas or lice, or they can be due to some internal complaint, like kidney disease, which obviously needs veterinary treatment.

TEETH

Teeth should be checked regularly for build-up of tartar, which can lead to gum disease (gingivitis) and the premature loss of teeth. If you suspect a problem, seek veterinary advice.

VOMITING

Vomiting in kittens may be serious, especially if the substance brought up resembles frothy, beaten egg whites, or is a bright yellow liquid. Vomiting accompanied by diarrhoea and a high temperature is a warning of some serious disease and the kitten needs urgent veterinary attention. If the kitten regurgitates undigested food you have no cause for alarm, it has merely eaten too much, or too quickly.

The most serious common illnesses likely to afflict cats and kittens – feline infectious enteritis and feline influenza ('cat flu') – can be effectively guarded against through immunization (see p.35).

Parasites

Fleas are disagreeable for both kitten and owner, but your veterinary surgeon can advise on the best treatment.

FLEAS

Fleas can be found on the best-kept kittens or cats. If you find some, first sprinkle your kitten carefully with flea powder, following the manufacturer's instructions. If this does not work satisfactorily, ask your veterinary surgeon for an anti-flea spray, and follow instructions carefully. It is important not to use an aerosol on a young kitten without first consulting your veterinary surgeon. Remember to de-flea bedding, carpets, and corners as well. It's no use treating the kitten or cat unless you thoroughly clean all the bedding and places where the kitten sleeps. Vacuuming the places where fleas can breed is every bit as important as treating the animal itself. If you think vacuuming hasn't solved the problem, ask your veterinary surgeon for a *surface* anti-flea spray, to be used only on floors and *never* on the kitten.

WORMS

Kittens and cats can become infected with two sorts of worms: round and tape. The roundworm is round in cross-section and measures 5–15cm/2–6in long. It can be a par-

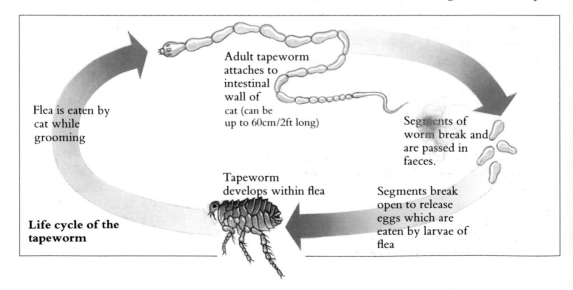

Flea is eaten by cat while grooming

Adult tapeworm attaches to intestinal wall of cat (can be up to 60cm/2ft long)

Segments of worm break and are passed in faeces.

Tapeworm develops within flea

Segments break open to release eggs which are eaten by larvae of flea

Life cycle of the tapeworm

Veterinary inspection of a sick Siamese. Note the visible third eyelid or haw.

ticular problem in kittens (which often pick up the worms from their mother), so they should be treated against roundworms at the age of four to six weeks.

Tapeworms are inclined to affect older animals and are caught from an intermediate host which, depending on the species of tapeworm, may be either a flea or a small rodent.

If you suspect your kitten has worms, ask your veterinary surgeon for the correct treatment.

LICE

Cats may also be affected by lice that are more difficult to see than fleas, although their white eggs, or nits, show up well, particularly on dark fur. Cats that constantly lick and bite themselves may be infested with lice, and should be taken to a veterinary surgeon for examination. The veterinary surgeon will be able to prescribe a good spray that will need to be used for at least a month.

Giving medicine

Kittens can sometimes be difficult patients when it comes to taking their medicine. However, once you know the basic guidelines to follow, administering medication can be much easier for both patient and owner.

Tablets   First, hold your kitten or cat securely. Put the animal on a non-slip surface. It is probably easiest if two people are on hand – one to administer the tablet, and the other to hold the cat's front legs, gently but firmly, from behind. Alternatively, you can wrap the kitten or cat securely in a blanket.

Next, put your left hand (if you are right-handed) on the top of the kitten's head, press your thumb and forefinger against the side of its jaws, and gently tilt the head back. The mouth should now be slightly open. With your right hand (which should, of course, be clean with fairly short fingernails) quickly put the tablet as far back down the kitten's throat as possible. Close up the mouth and gently stroke the back of the throat to help the pill move down the gullet A very large tablet can always be broken up into smaller pieces.

Liquid medicine   Follow the procedure above and gently pull out the cheek to form a pouch into which medicine can be trickled from a spoon, or small plastic syringe, a few drops at a time. Do be sure, though, to give the kitten enough time to swallow.

Ear drops   Hold the kitten's head to one side and insert the drops using the applicator supplied. Gently stroke behind the ear to help the drops penetrate. Clean away any surplus drops from the ear with great care.

Eye drops   Hold the kitten's head back and apply the eye drops to the inner corner of the eye using the applicator supplied. Keep the head back for a while to allow the drops to cover the whole surface of the eye.

First aid

In an emergency do not rush to the veterinary surgeon without first checking that someone will be there. Phone first. There are several things you can do while waiting for professional help.

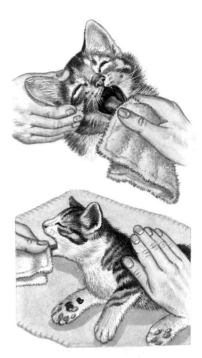

First, make sure the kitten is breathing without obstruction. This might necessitate clearing the airway by pulling the tongue forward – hold it with a handkerchief and take care not to get bitten.

Any major bleeding should be staunched by placing a clean, folded handkerchief over the wound and pressing firmly enough to stop the blood flow.

Shock is countered by keeping the kitten as quiet as possible, preferably in a darkened room, and as warm as possible by covering with a blanket, applying a well-wrapped hot-water bottle or raising the temperature of the room overall.

To apply artificial respiration the kitten should ideally be on its right side, with head and neck extended and the tongue pulled forward. Place your hand over the ribs just behind the shoulder blade, compress the chest cavity, then relax the pressure, allowing the chest to expand naturally. Repeat at five- to six-second intervals.

Take great care in moving an injured kitten. If it seems that the kitten has sustained a fracture, avoid moving the kitten at all if possible. Never attempt to apply a splint or bandage, and wait calmly for help to arrive. If, for example, after a car accident, a kitten must be moved straight away, slide it carefully on to a tray and use this as a stretcher. Where no fracture is suspected, use a secure carrier in order to transport the kitten to the veterinary surgery. A strong grocery box can make a good emergency carrier if the sides are pierced for ventilation and the top tied down.

Your questions answered

I think my kitten has worms, but how can I tell?

Many kittens have roundworm from birth and in the early stages do not show many symptoms except perhaps a pot belly. Sometimes the worms, looking like pieces of very thin white string, are seen in the faeces. It is important not to let a kitten go untreated as a heavy infestation will interfere with digestion, and the kitten will not thrive as it should. Consequently, 'worming' should be routine and your veterinary surgeon will advise on suitable dosage.

Another type of worm found in a cat's digestive system is the tapeworm, and its presence can often be detected by segments of the worm, resembling grains of rice, seen around the anus. Medicine for roundworm will not kill a tapeworm, and treatment should be given under veterinary supervision.

When playing in the garden, our four-month-old kitten often dashes under the car parked in the drive and emerges with streaks of oil along her back. How can it be removed safely?

Oil must be removed from the kitten's coat without delay as it is highly toxic if absorbed through the coat or tongue. Any lumps or thick patches should be carefully wiped from the coat with toilet tissue, then the residue washed off with a mild household detergent. Once the oil is removed, rinse all traces of detergent from the coat and dry the kitten thoroughly. If the kitten is heavily coated in oil, waste no time in taking it to the veterinary surgeon. Wipe away as much of the substance as possible and make sure that the kitten does not lick its coat by wrapping its body in a towel.

Kittens should be kept away from oil, grease and wet paint. Garages are dangerous places for young kittens – there are sharp tools and the possibility of the kitten licking anti-freeze which could prove lethal. Kittens are also likely to crawl up into the engine of a vehicle, or on to a tyre and out of sight. If the vehicle is started before the kitten is discovered it could result in tragedy.

I know my kitten must be expected to claw the furniture, but is there anything I can do to discourage him, or will he just grow out of it?
Cats will always need to sharpen their claws, and they will not 'naturally' be able to differentiate between an oak tree and an antique sideboard! However, they can and should be trained from kittenhood not to claw certain things. Provide a suitable scratching post (see p. 31) and each time your kitten attempts to scratch the furniture, clap your hands together and say 'No' sharply. Then encourage him to use the scratching post instead by placing his forepaws on the surface and making slight scratching movements with them. With patience he should soon learn.

I worry when my little kitten gets stuck up a tree. What is the best way to get her down?
Climbing as high as possible seems to be a favourite activity with cats; many will happily spend the day on the ridge of a roof or stretched out on a lofty branch. Just because your kitten does not come down doesn't mean she can't – but she may be intimidated by a sea of upturned, calling faces below her. Even if she is mewing and would obviously like to come down, it is probably best to let her work out her own plan of descent. With her highly developed sense of balance she is unlikely to fall. You may safely leave her there for several hours and, if left alone, perhaps with a plate of strong-smelling food at the base of the tree, curiosity or hunger (or greed!) will usually be sufficient enticement.

If you do decide to climb up after her, take a zip-up bag or strong pillow case into which you can pop her before bringing her down.

As my kitten is infested with fleas, we have bought some flea powder. But will it be dangerous if she licks her fur after the powder has been applied – would a spray have been safer?
A veterinary-recommended spray is generally more effective than a powder, but either must be applied *exactly* in accordance with the manufacturer's instructions, taking great care to avoid the kitten's eyes and genital region. After application, keep the kitten amused while the product does its work, then brush and comb the coat to remove dead fleas, débris and the residue of the insecticide.

Life history

Scientific name	*Felis catus*
Gestation period	63 days (approx.)
Litter size	3–5 (average)
Birth weight	90 g/3 oz–140 g/5 oz
Eyes open	10 days
Weaning age	42–56 days
Weaning weight	500 g/1 lb 2 oz– 650 g/1 lb 7 oz
Puberty	120–180 days
Adult weight	males 3.5 kg/8 lb– 5.9 kg/13 lb females 2.25 kg/5 lb– 3 kg/7 lb
Best age to breed	12+ months
Oestrus (or season)	repeatedly in season Jan–Oct unless mated
Duration of oestrus	7–14 days
Retire from breeding	males 10 years females 8 years
Life expectancy	12–16 years

Record card

Record sheet for your own kitten

Name

Date of birth
(actual or estimated)

Breed   Sex

Colour/description

(photograph or portrait)

Feeding notes

Medical record

Date of neutering operation

Veterinary surgeon's name   Surgery hours

Practice address

Tel. no.

Vaccination record for [kitten's name]

Vaccination at age 10-12 weeks   date   Age of kitten   Veterinary surgeon
          feline infectious enteritis

                    feline influenza

Booster injections, as recommended by Veterinary surgeon: dates:

Index